"Cliff Burns' books belong on anyone's five-foot shelf of essential reading, lodged snugly between Borges and Burroughs."

Stefan Dziemianowicz

"The writing here is clever, thought-provoking, and easily on par with anything else in the CanLit section of any major bookstore. Burns deserves to be more widely known than he is, though it would be tough to find a Canadian author with a more dedicated fan base."

Ottawa Review of Books

"Burns writes like Hitchcock directs, producing gooseflesh without monsters. And *that* is the scariest writing there is."

Factsheet Five (USA)

Notebooks:
2010 – 2020

Cliff Burns

Cover design: Chris Kent
Interior layout: Megan McCullough

Published by Black Dog Press (blackdogpress@yahoo.ca)

Printed by: Lightning Source

ISBN: 978-0-9938721-8-1 (Print)
        978-0-9938721-9-8 (Ebook)

Also by Cliff Burns:

Electric Castles: A Book of Urban Legends (stories)
Mouth: Rants and Routines (E-book only)
The Algebra of Inequality (poetry)
Righteous Blood (novellas)
Sex & Other Acts of the Imagination (stories)
Disloyal Son
Exceptions and Deceptions (stories)
New and Selected Poems (1985-2011)
Stromata: Prose Works (1992-2011)
The Last Hunt
Of the Night
So Dark the Night
The Reality Machine (stories)

BLACK DOG PRESS

"Despair is a sin against the imagination."
Greta Ehrlich

"Conscience is the face of the soul."
Thomas Merton

"God is at home. We are in the far country."
Meister Eckhart

"Man has a grueling evolution behind him, and the subconscious bears the mark of the beast."
John Bowle

Contents

Introduction

I've never been able to keep a regular journal and maybe that's a good thing.

After all, it isn't as if my life is incredibly interesting or inspiring—to be honest, the opposite is true.

How can I accurately depict for you just how utterly boring and uneventful it is in my little bubble of reality, the depressing monotony of my days?

Each morning I wake up, cross the hallway from our bedroom to my office, sit down and commence work. And that's pretty much *it*. There's very little variation from that routine, nothing to break a cycle that hasn't changed much in thirty+ years.

Wouldn't it be nice if my dull, sedentary existence was my way of observing Flaubert's famous advice to artists, to be "steady and well-ordered in your life so that you can be fierce and original in your work"?

Sorry, folks, but that just isn't the case.

And what about this book you now hold in your hands, what sort of insights can be gained *vis a vis* life, creativity, spirituality, philosophy, whatever, from some obscure, cult writer of modest talent, limited readership and no ambition beyond putting words on paper that do justice to the beauty and evocative power of language? What do I have to say that would be of the slightest interest to you or anybody else?

Honestly, I don't have a ready answer to either query.

All I can tell you is that for the past decade whenever the impulse has struck me, I reach for a thin, Moleskine notebook and jot down a few errant thoughts or authorial asides. It doesn't happen regularly and sometimes weeks pass before something occurs to me and I scribble a new entry.

I don't know what compels me to do so, have no idea why I have continued this practice for ten bloody years.

Further on this point, I make no claims that my observations are in any way original or unique to me, or that my mini-epiphanies will resonate with any sentient creature possessing even a modicum of intelligence (how's that for a sales pitch).

I am not a wise man, philosopher or aspiring theologian. More like a seeker, insatiably curious but lacking the means or mental dexterity to truly address the complexity and grandeur of the surrounding universe.

I guess you could call me an autodidact, no formal training or education in any field but, that said, I have a mind that adamantly refuses to be hemmed in by constricting horizons or cowed by a specific god or dogma or worldview that will not submit itself to close examination.

If you're willing to make allowances for my lack of academic credentials, plus a lifelong tendency to brood over the weirdest things, well, perhaps you might find something of value here, an insight or reflection that rings true to you and provides grist for further ruminations.

That, I think, is the best I can hope for, a fragile, likely untenable aspiration that permits me, despite my misgivings, to release this odd little tome into the world (where it will undoubtedly sink without a trace).

I believe my motivations to be sincere and heartfelt—ah, but you see, that's the trouble with *hubris*, it's so good at affecting beneficence and sagaciousness it sometimes gets mistaken for perspicacity or perhaps even, God help me, wisdom.

C.B.
(March, 2021)

Book I

I want to forget all I know, begin again at absolute zero;
knowledge can be fatal to creativity. Self-reflection sometimes
an excuse for indulgence.
Avoid patterns, formulae, common wisdom.
Play the fool, paint my face, run away and join the circus.

If not now, when?
Are you afraid of the burden that comes with being a messenger?
Place your trust where it rightfully belongs.
Surrender, submit; first prostration, then prayer.

I don't want to die until I see what the future brings.

Like Alice, on the other side of the looking glass, shrieking,
palms pressed against an unbreakable barrier.

Heat death, devouring even the stones.

It will begin in Yemen/
spreading out from there/
they're building a killer bug/
releasing it into the air.

I don't suppose it matters/
the sun will explode one day/
we live and cry and love/
and then we fade away.

Death: insensate, oblivious to all but the Divine.

Babel separates us. We need a common language, a vernacular that unites us, otherwise we are doomed. Remember: our myths *always* end in apocalypse.

Ours is the last generation of plenty.
We've spent our inheritance,
living on borrow time,
breathing our children's air.

Touching the zeitgeist
the reception loud and clear;
tapping into the collective mood
channeling mortal dread.

A few trillion brain cells, the sum total of all I am at this particular moment.

Deny me everything but a voice.

I cheerfully murder first drafts, throttling my offspring before they've drawn more than two or three sips of breath.

What next? What does my Muse have in store for me now? Never what I'm expecting. I've stopped guessing. I swore an oath of fealty. I have no right to complain.

Just don't leave me paralyzed, pen forever poised above the page.

Inner dialogue:
What should I make of this?
That inspiration is fickle.
Should I persevere?
Only if you must.

I'm happy—so what am I trying to escape?

Automatic writing is a seismograph of the unconscious,
recording tremors and tectonic upheavals, continental plates
grating against each other. And, always, pressure from beneath,
heat and destructive forces threatening to break through.

We are the next mass extinction.

The world's oldest orphan never ceases yearning for a parent
to love them and take them home.

Inevitably, the gears will grind to a stop, a shriek of tortured
machinery, death knell of civilization.

We're turning inward, abandoning vision for advantage.
Stupid and self-absorbed, never thinking beyond *now*.

They aren't telling us everything (trying to avoid panic).
Something bad is about to happen, our world changing
between breaths.

I am ennobled by love, owe any grace I've achieved to your
sweet ministrations.

You are an article of my faith, my favorite gospel.

You have never given the slightest credence to despair.

Do I want to be the victim or the crime?
Steal what I must or starve while the greediest among us thrive?

I'm constantly making excuses for myself, inventing a
rationale for non-compliance and failure.

Hiding behind politeness, obsequiousness, concealing the
inner coward.

Are you reading this in some distant tomorrow?
Do my words carry the same intended meaning?
Does the Earth still warily orbit the sun?
And your eyes, are they *real* behind that gaze?

There are hidden meanings, portents and sigils.
That notch in the tree, a warning to wise eyes.

"No one remembers the Armenians."
The terrible consequences of human indifference.

Static.
Nothing getting through today.
Turn off the receiver, wind in the aerial.
Save your batteries.
Keep watching the skies.

Smug, because I haven't suffered enough.

Today my brain seems slow, common, nothing to distinguish it from the rest of the herd. Where are the insights? Why does everything appear so mundane and *ordinary*?

No major peccadilloes to report.
Not that I'm blameless, just that I lack the guts to act on my urges.

History must have its scapegoats, even as the vast majority of the guilty escape unscathed.

I'll find your heartstrings, even if I have to *cut* for them.

You are Polaris, constant and faithful, a beacon and guiding light.

The findings are unequivocal: as a human being I am, at best, nominal. Need to show great improvement for any chance of promotion.

Keep the home fires burning so the survivors can find their way back.

Fear the corporate mindset.
We know that, collectively, human beings are capable of great evil.

Does it matter?
Won't darkness prevail in the end?
Can any light be sustained when the sun and stars are burning their days?

Most people die of old age.
The will to survive is that strong.

I'm forty-seven.
An old man in Sierra Leone.

How often have I been severely tested?
Am I brave or only pretending?

In summation, what am I trying to communicate?
That *this* isn't all there is.

Keep pushing this pen.
Like a boulder up a mountain.

Does a dead man care if his words live on?
Does pride have a place in Heaven?

I am redeemed by my love of this good woman.

The world will never be safe.
If necessary, we invent our enemies.

I collect books.
Afraid they'll disappear.
Lost, like the Library of Alexandria.
Fooling myself I'll have time to read them.
Fussing over my charges like a medieval monk.

Perhaps, like Sappho, only fragments will survive.
Enough to sustain the myth, hinting at what was lost.

No one lives blamelessly.
Even Jesus was guilty of treading on ants.

There's something, a message flickering in and out.
"...*come in...over...*"

Some walk in tune with the Universe, their souls
encompassing infinity.

"Let there be light!"
(Four simple words.)

He had a particular quality of cruelty that made him ideally
suited for the work.
A high tolerance for inflicting pain without the slightest
twinge of conscience or remorse.
Their screams didn't bother him, a clash of metal on a noisy
factory floor.
He got used to it.
And he said it didn't take long.

Seeking a signal, despite the background noise.
Takes patience and a good ear.
An unshakable conviction there's someone else out there,
anxious to make contact, lonely as we are.

They never talked about it when they got back from the moon.
But they *all* heard it.

There you are. Why are you crying? I didn't mean it and, anyway, I was angry. My words were poorly chosen. I can see they hurt you. Forgive my insensitivity, but I honestly didn't think you'd care.

What do we do with the bodies?
There's too many to bury or burn.
It's a question of public health.
And the dogs can only eat so much.

I want to think with perfect clarity.
I've muddled my faculties with drugs and drink.
There's something I've been missing.
Life beyond my aquarium mind.

My bad habits are starting to get the best of me.

Doodles and botched computations.
Working my way toward an all-encompassing Grand Theory of Everything.

It might be superstition, but I never flip the calendar until the first day of the new month.

There is precious little of anything left.
Sound FX: straw dredging up the last remnants of milk at the bottom of the glass.

Health. Happiness. Wisdom.
That's it.

Dead: a permanent cessation, welcome oblivion.

It keeps building, an inner pressure 'til I'm bursting at the seams.

I didn't understand a word he was saying but his pain was
so evident I nodded and made sympathetic sounds. His
experiences beyond expression; even a common language
wouldn't have helped.

The lights go out, all over the world.
And it gets cold very, very quickly once it's dark.

Will it happen all at once or gradually peter out?

Will I live to see my grandchildren starving?

I have the misfortune (luck?) of being self-analytical.

I'll include Paris in my Beatitudes, see if it gets me there.

When the last days loom one should retreat into silence, an
inner conversation that beggars language.

An accumulation of detail.
An apt description of life.

Fewer and fewer Christmas cards every year.
A spate of disappearances.
Fill out a Missing Person report.
Put out an A.P.B.
Searching for traces of everyone I used to know.

I've been keeping secrets out of shame, which requires lies and subterfuge, evasion, distraction, defensiveness, a constant state of preparedness, fingers torn and aching from trying to fill the cracks in the dike.

Not giving in to fear, that's the hardest part.

Infidels, apostates, blasphemers, knowingly committing treason against God.

Why should Lucifer bow to the likes of us?

Expending so much time, so many pages, resources, pursuing a chimera.

Apply to all things: is this indispensable?

Economic forces supersede mere humanity.

What happens when the last vestiges of the soul are snuffed out? What fills the resulting void?

I hate to harp on this, but I don't seem to be getting any closer to perfection.

Get it all down.
Exorcize those voices.

My secret identity as the most boring man who ever lived.

Strong, tactile memories of the way her skin felt, the whorl of nipple that rose to my touch.

"The living will envy the dead."
What about those of us who have neglected to live?

A life largely devoid of incident.

How far down dare I go?
What will my sensibilities endure?

Pure substance, bubbling up from the Omphalos.

My personal archive stored in rectangular cartons (like coffins).

These scraps of paper, all that remain of me.
Take them to the stars, will you, plant them on some faraway world.

I can go an entire year without listening to my favorite musicians…and then play nothing else for a solid week.

Emotional upheavals and traumas are like black holes, distorting the space/time continuum, warping and twisting things beyond recognition.

Who will be staring out through my eyes tomorrow?

Regain focus; quiet the mind, tune out ephemera, nattering radio voices.
Wait, pen poised.
Wait. *Wait…*

Time to start thinking deeply about critical matters. My mind wanders; shortened attention span, chronic indolence, showing my monkey roots.

Who benefits from our becoming more and more stupid?

The internet: O.B.S.
One big store.
Conceived and created by capitalism.
An ersatz town hall or public square, the illusion of freedom, community…
…but really devised in order to steal intellectual property rights, free programming for paid advertisements.

How to spend my remaining days.
Is there still time for revelation?

I could weep.

"Shoegazer" music.
How apt.
Lately I've been staring holes in the toes of my slippers.

The sun exploded four and a half minutes ago.
What shall we do while we wait?

Comrade, save the last bullet for your commanding officer.

Ozymandias, every single one of us.

Words on paper, committing to the page the sensations of being alive, the extravagant luxury of each drawn breath.

A life of silence, contemplation and reading.
Would that be so bad?

A long litany of "might-have-beens".

How many failures turn out to be posthumous geniuses?
(Very few, as it happens, the proportion dispiritingly low.)

Heliopause: where the sun runs out.

The Seven Wonders of the ancient world were meant to last forever.

One last revelation—stepping through an unlocked door and…

Whistleblowers = good citizens = enemies of the state

History: opening the account books to shareholder scrutiny.

Giving someone the "Assange treatment": ruining their reputation, inventing crimes, discrediting the messenger.

They've planted lies with friendly media outlets. Remotely installed unspeakable things on my hard drive. Hacked my bank accounts, maxed out my credit cards. I've stepped on the wrong toes and now the smear campaign has commenced, a remorseless strategy to dissuade free thinkers, erasing the last traces of dissent.

Speed of thought: exponentially faster than the speed of light.

Blacken someone's name until it's no longer visible.

Happiness is a well-appointed cage.

Movement within the bonfires.

Freedom is a constant state of exhilarating terror.

Hope dies just before the soul.

Dullard. What wisdom or insights do you have to impart?
You are having one of your "off" days. Clumsy and stupid.
Nothing you say or do comes out right. Go back to bed, pull
the covers over your useless head. Call in sick, tell them you
are too ridiculous to come to work today.

Sometimes I die in my dreams.
So far, I've seen no evidence of an afterlife.

It's only recently that I've started trusting myself again.

All philosophy is useless.
Science and logic do not apply.
Magic rules the universe; alchemy, escaped from the page.

Time's arrow/
once unleashed/
flies straight and true/
never failing to find/
its intended target.

"I.C.U."
this is all that's left
existence pared down to
the bare minimum;
life support
intubated
gasping for each breath
hallucinating a universe
filled with familiar faces

nature sounds
birdsong
recorded for posterity
before they're gone

"endangered"
confined to museums
those creepy tableaux
painted dioramas
glass bead eyes
stiff, frozen poses

If I stop sedating myself will the world collapse in on me
with crushing force, my eyeballs bursting out of their sockets,
brains leaking from my ears?

And now a word from our sponsor:
At the end of the universe
take the first left after the lights
follow the one-armed man
into the woods where
you will meet a tall dark
stranger who will explain
everything in time for
the first commercial break

War, like any good ad campaign, requires a catchy tag line.
"Shock and awe" merely another take on "new and improved".

Why did they build it in the shape of a pentagon?

Vast storerooms where they keep the stuff.
You need a special key card to gain admittance.
No numbers on the doors and if you have to ask, you don't
belong there.

There is a group of people who conspire to create
conspiracy theories.

I believe it's possible to die from boredom.
I've seen it happen.

A miracle or weird coincidence?
Same thing.

I am frightened by deep holes. Crevasses, cracks in the world
going all the way down to Hell.

Recurring dream: killing someone and burying them in the
front yard. A six-foot by three-foot hole in the lawn, an
obvious grave. Only a matter of time before a squad car pulls
up, two serious looking men extricating themselves from the
vehicle, striding up the walk.

At times, my fantasies threaten to overwhelm me.

The last drink from the bottle.
The one you thought you were saving but couldn't.
(later)
Years afterward, a disillusioned Quixote became a lush,
tipping at gin mills.

Deemed unfit to serve.
4-F for flat feet and a poor attitude.

When I feel undeserving, petty, insignificant (as I do now), I have a hard time meeting their eyes.

The difference between
     "fact" and "truth"
     "art" and "morality"
     "hope" and "expectation"
     "regret" and "remorse"
     "civilized" and "sane"
     "devotion" and "love"
     "science" and "reality"
     "poor" and "impoverished"
     "writer" and "author"
     "image" and "man"
     "mind" and "brain"
     "comprehension" and "understanding"
     "conclusion" and "resolution"
     "naked" and "exposed"
     "justice" and "retribution"
     "wisdom" and "tact"
     "symbol" and "metaphor"
     "religion" and "god"
     "eternal" and "infinite"
     "glory" and "grace"

They have run out of lies.
They've started repeating themselves.
We can anticipate their falsehoods verbatim.
Predict a declaration of war before a single shot is fired.

The good times are over, the piper waiting to be paid.
You've mortgaged your future selves, smothered your
grandchildren in their beds.

What else have I withheld?
What is there left to tell?
Are there any bones still unpicked?

So many regrets and no one I can share them with.

Determined to be a refusenik, a gypsy, a faggot, a Jew.
Anything that separates me from the obliging herd.

God is dead, Creation his death throes.

I am not a baby anymore and, to my horror, no longer buoyant.

Who shall I pray to today?

Can you ever fall too far and escape even the possibility of Grace?

Here, certainty reigns.
A Newtonian universe, sterile, cold and precise.

Quips and aphorisms: is that all my thoughts amount to?

The Old Testament: scary campfire stories.

You buy things to make yourself happy.
Everybody deserves to be happy.
You read that somewhere.

At times like this, I have a hard time working up enough
energy to give a fuck.

Be an iconoclast, like Don Glen Vliet or the Butthole Surfers.
A small, rabid following sharing the same strange wavelength.

Hint: space is *not* curved and time nothing more than an
artificial construct.

I have a secret fear I might be inadequate, if not expendable.

My warrantee just ran out and there's something wrong with
my eyes.

Here we are once again.

I'm told you're not satisfied with the accommodations.

It took Ethel Rosenberg twenty minutes to die.

Why can't they turn plastic back into petroleum?
How come cars can't run on empty milk jugs and human waste?

Effluvia: pretty word for bad smell.

Am I a computer simulation?
That would explain a lot...

An herbal remedy to make me more virile.
No doubt watered by the same reservoir that nourishes the
Fountain of Youth.

Commercials: capitalist propaganda, endlessly repeated.

Voters: willing accomplices to fraud.

I live in terror of being a man of no consequence.
Like you, Dad.

I am only a witness, never a willing participant.

I talk too much and give myself away.

"Love? What is it? Most natural pain killer what there is. LOVE."
(William S. Burroughs' last journal entry)

Stop buying.
Stop feeding the machine that's feeding on *you*.
You are, after all, what eats you.

Sex simultaneously dignifies and humbles. How is that possible?

Here it comes.
God, help me.

Philip K. Dick was a prophet.
One day, they'll name a religion after him (and, somewhere, Phil will be laughing his ass off).

Science informs us we're inconsequential; religion assures us we're blessed.

We must use the mechanisms and institutions of democracy to combat the depredations of capitalism.

What have we forgotten? What would we remember should we ever fully awaken?

Werner Herzog's "ecstatic truth".

They couldn't have faked the moon landing, we would've seen the wires!

Fight paradox with poetry.

I am plagued by nostalgia—am I the only one who remembers?

I want to live off the grid, under the radar, down a road that doesn't exist on any map. Left to my own devices, waving to you from a sagging porch.

Every so often I wish I could descend the evolutionary ladder, find a place not complicated by reason.

Reduced in the end to wordless, strangled breaths, like a character out of Beckett.

I am miserly with my affections, meting them out like favors to my personal court.

Forbidden Planet: all that Krell machinery, waiting for a single spark of hate.

The scariest people are the ones inside you.

Skewed statistics and a cowed media conceal the identities of the real criminals and malefactors in our society: supposedly law-abiding citizens, Chamber of Commerce members, paragons of the community, immune from prosecution, invulnerable by common consent.

A quick reminder that we are *all* victims of brain chemistry.

I feel grey.

Avoid the steady state!
Frustrate the algorithms!

"Sanctify your life." (*Les Miserables*)

Chemical filters to dilute experience, the pain(s) of existence.

I am an ancient addict.

How much more can we endure? Denied hope, where do we find the courage to confront the boundless Void?

How many times must you immolate yourself before finally putting out the match?

George Harrison: gifted, fragile, prone to sinning, saint with a stiff prick.

And what's wrong with a good, old-fashioned *om mani padme om*?

Lose attachments, old standards of measurement.

Brushed by the ineffable, a sensation resembling nothing I've experienced before.

Tonight, I feel like a ghost haunting my home.

A reliance on miracles implies a lack of faith.

Make coherent some small region of the universe and call it *home*.

"All things are nothing to me." (Max Stirner)
That level of scorn for existence can only have its origins in the trenches.

It's always the buzzing of flies that tells us where to look.

Can a melody be discerned within the cacophony?
That is the purpose of faith.

To be dogged by a young man's uncertainties at this point in
my life.

I think I will always regard the world with the sidelong
glance of an absurdist.

Birdsong and lawnmowers: the soundtrack of Ray Bradbury.

Don't let me die unacknowledged.
Better scorned and vilified than that.

We seek paragons and call them *saints*.
An iconography of the virtuous; bloodless and exempt
from reproach.

Recalling Joyce's "silence, exile, cunning".

The universe, apparently, a bubble of reality.
So, who's holding the pin?

Jungian theory: untold millions inside us, seeking to make
their presence known.

Marring this blank page with malice aforethought.

Old enough to know better (hair growing from my ears).

The perfect ending: a culmination or new beginning?

How do you portray nonexistence?

Gen-o-cide.
So easy to pronounce.

The women and children too.

I must have offended God, the words won't come.

Kept waiting, a reminder of my low station.

In limbo, like Schrodinger's cat.
Impatient for someone to open the lid.

The peace of mind of an unrepentant heathen.

Richard Dawkins refers to the "blind, pitiless indifference of the universe". Which perfectly fits my conception of Hell.

There I go again, ranting about my latest bugbear. Note the look of bemusement on my listener's face. Too polite to walk away…

Offering this disclaimer/qualifier: *Ecce Homo*.

The end of the world: when they steal your coat, ignoring the proffered money.

Where are you?
Why can't I see you?
How do I know you're real?

Radical politics: because everything else has failed.

Ecocide: narcissism running wild.

If I'm a good person it's because I love more passionately than I hate.

Somehow we find each other over and over again.

A nightmare in the sense that there's no logical rhyme or reason.

Paradox. Enigma. Conundrum.
Words for what baffles us.

It's getting harder to hide my allegiances.

Alain Badiou equates capitalists with gangsters.
What would our local Chamber of Commerce say to *that*?

We must choose our heroes and villains with care.

Obdurate. Implacable.
Words that do not *yield*.

Fear: a survival mechanism grafted on to the amygdala.

Hellscape: the environs of the damned.

Time to permanently shed the "white man's burden".

It is impossible to live up to your own standards.

A hypocrite and phony every time I open my mouth.

The tribes are lining up.

All for a cup of milk and a few slices of bread.

Go underground, communicate via *samizdat*.

A tendency to weep at the futility of it all.

Condemned to watch it fall.

Cassandra: what she saw every time she closed her eyes…

The awful things we do to each other, inexcusable, even as history.

They might paint you pure gold, prostrate themselves before you, but you'll *never* be a god.

Surely the Easter Islanders knew what they were doing.

A plague on *all* our houses, punishing us indiscriminately.

"And I only am escaped alone to tell thee…"

Continuing a long line of drunks, thugs and non-entities.

The wisdom it takes to shut up and listen.

Anomie: an epidemic of otherness.

Domesticated, like an animal, a slave.

Flowers of evil (sown in toxic soil).

The "long emergency", during which so many will die.

"I is not I." (Rimbaud)
Isn't that the case for all of us?

Trying to conceive of a world without a strong central government, basic services, reliable infrastructure, a guaranteed food supply. Is this what they mean by dystopia or merely the inevitable byproducts of late-stage capitalism?

Autarky: reason defeated by fear.

"…history moves in a single direction and that direction is forward." (Kan Kalfus, *Equilateral*)

War: unreasonable use of force in an unjust cause.

I don't want to die unfulfilled.

Outwardly hard-working but, by nature, slothful and easily distracted.

A long history of wakeful, restive nights.
(Guilty conscience, maybe?)

Sin: not merely an impious deed but an impious thought.

The past: stillborn.
Present: heavy with possibility.
Future: squalling, messy, unpredictable.

Jesus wept, and who can blame him?

James Howard Kunstler's "mutilated urbanism".

I remember little of my childhood except what I've invented.

Raised by wolves.
A feral upbringing, the runt of the litter.

We're smart monkeys, good at keeping our cages tidy
and organized.

Martyr: a masochist by any other name.

Prophets
(to take our measure)
Messiahs
(to deliver the verdict)

Granted life, through no fault of my own.

There is a certain amount of residual shame in almost every
human act.

I would
she wouldn't
so we didn't

By attrition then, if not by accident or misadventure.

The dreams of God: withheld from us out of consideration for our delicate sensibilities.

All the best idols have fallen, leaving in their stead demi-urges, lesser gods. Poor substitutes for their illustrious forebears.

When the world is moving too fast and your reality filters can no longer cope.

A familiar sense of impending disaster.

Sustained by a steady diet of denial, hope, fervent prayers.

Family reunions: aging faces, thickening bodies, conflicting memories.

There is no medical name for what afflicts me. It is a disease of the *soul*.

What makes you think the future even exists?

Dogmatic: paging through a holy text, seeking confirmation of something you already know.

I think we each bear a price tag and somewhere in the world there is a person who knows our true worth down to the last penny.

I could honestly tell them I sometimes hear voices.

Remove the fourth wall, confront them with what they've wrought.

Waiting for an epiphany (yes, I'm that desperate).

God has moved on to his *next* creation.

Einstein's *gedankenexperiments* (genius at play).

Ghosts of empire wail the loudest.

In short, I try to make the incomprehensible palatable.

I've kept my end of the bargain and up until now have suffered in silence. I know I occasionally need to be humbled, but this time I sense real malice.

Loneliness is the ultimate mind-altering drug.

A mailman is always announced by barking dogs.

Magic and rituals predate organized religion by millennia.

Reading Calvino's *Castle of Crossed Destinies* and one passage stands out, like it's highlighted: "In writing, what speaks is what is repressed". Sherron and I discuss this in relation to my work. What am I repressing or trying to confront obliquely? The powerlessness of my childhood? The betrayals of those closest me? Or something else, an incident or interval I've mercifully forgotten.

Memory is the ultimate unreliable narrator.

Victor Serge's "unity of word and deed".

"I have found that the writer cannot even exist in our decomposing, modern societies without accommodating himself to interests that forcibly limit his horizons and mutilate his sincerity." (Victor Serge, *Memoirs of a Revolutionary*)

A revolution is never defeated, merely co-opted.

Avoiding the arrogance of certainty.

Truth is whatever our sensibilities and dispositions can abide.

What Russell Brand calls "the haphazard data of biography".

A desire to leave this world richer with laughter and poorer in tears.

Scientists speaking without a trace of humility of "assisting evolution".

"…interludes between films left him in an intolerable depressive limbo." (Georgia Brown, on Rainer Werner Fassbinder)

My spirit, contained within my soul.

The Ten Commandments: proscriptive *and* prescriptive.

For lonely people, the universe is Ptolemaic, revolving around *them*.

A sickening desire to please.
Fawning, when solicitude would suffice.

There is no room for sentiment in a full-blown mystical experience.

Spectacle, in lieu of content.

What am I?
Vital energy animating living flesh.
What is my purpose?
To observe, experience, record; Akashic telemetry…

Eternity is a long, long time.

Sherron and I: a love that strains credulity.

Spirit precedes—and ultimately transcends—mere flesh.

I have terrible thoughts.
Some days I have no desire to be kind or tolerant.
My mindset positively genocidal.
The stupid, directionless rage of the worst Nazi.

Skepticism can be a kind of secular fundamentalism. By rabidly denying the existence of *spirit*, what are we trying to suppress or extinguish within ourselves? We can refuse to engage with Mystery, but at what cost?

Avoiding the tendency to turn on myself.

In any artistic endeavor, sentiment is the equivalent of an artificial sweetener, extraneous and bathetic.

No more days left to waste.

Death: a reaping for what you have sown.

How long before all this inactivity makes me *soft*?

My God, people, there's a world to be saved!

The universe is observed.
The universe reacts to observation.
And then, presumably, it observes right back.

Doesn't every religion have an apocalypse doctrine?
Even Buddha dreamed *gotterdammerung*.

Hallowed ground, wherever you stand.

Atheism possesses its own iconography, hierarchy of saints.
(St. Hitchens, St. Dawkins, St. Russell…)

All ghosts originate from the future.

I still pout: a little brat until the day I die.

Opt out of the narrative they're writing you.

I want to live on Mars.

God preserve us from those claiming to know God's will.

Alexander Trocchi asks why God prefers Abel, the butcher,
over Cain, the farmer.

Too little praise, too much condemnation.

No one kicking down my door or throwing me into the back
of a van, disappearing me. But…isn't it worse to be unnoticed,
unacknowledged, not deemed worthy of scrutiny?

Determined to suffer 'til my last ragged breath.

In the vast, virtually infinite universe, there's only *one* you.
Which, any way you look at it, makes you a miracle.
Unprecedented and irreplaceable.
There. Feeling any better?

We conceal the best, most admirable aspects of ourselves, refusing to share those qualities with an apathetic or hostile world.

When you actively seek to disrupt the narratives others live by, you have to expect a violent response.

I'm lost without you, my inner compass spinning uselessly.

J.G. Ballard, writing in *High Rise* of a "future that had already taken place and was now exhausted".

Is it wrong to hate a hater?

Gifted at the art of subterfuge, secretive almost by instinct.

Faith: restricting our options for our own good.

There is no evidence someone named Moses ever existed. Does that negate the enduring value of the Ten Commandments?

Would life be more tolerable if it was accompanied by a catchy musical score?

Each year I am more sensitive to the cold. I dread winter, insulating myself against its pervasive, relentless chill.

Nakba, or catastrophe.
(Cry for Palestine.)

Memoricide: murdering the past in cold blood.

Still clinging to hope, for the sake of the children.

Having exhausted all appeals.
With eternity staring me in the face.
Throwing myself on the mercy of the court.
Pleading ignorance, disavowing all responsibility.

Play dumb (it's worked before).

Bitten by a flu bug; tetchy and listless.
Secretly looking forward to being pampered, fussed over.
Meanwhile, pretending to resent all the care and attention.

Mirror: primitive Turing Test.

Mental illness: dogged by an annoying, incessant laugh track.

A feeling of futility, the worst kind of impotence. Not even
able to feign arousal, the slightest stirring of tumescence.

My art and my cock: intimately connected.
In fact, inseparable.

Sometimes humility must be *imposed*.

Keep quiet.
Walk softly.
There are wolves about.

Referring to one of his searing pieces, Pederecki said as he composed it he imagined taking an ice pick to Stalin (the weapon of choice, it seems, when it comes to dispatching Soviet-era leaders).

Can one wear a red star or sport a hammer and sickle without dishonoring the many victims of those symbols?

Inside me, a rock star, a diva, a despot, howling to be set free.

God: anthropomorphizing Creation.

My mind turning inward, like a collapsing star.

The *Gospel of Judas* and Jesus' evident contempt for his disciples ("the Twelve").

The more we observe the universe, the further it retreats from us.

I've had a number of close calls—how many lives do I have left?

We live in futility, die in confusion (or is it the other way around?).

Reiterating Plato: aren't you tired of living in an intellectual grotto, frightened of shadows?

Calculate randomness, call it quantum physics.
Quantify Creation, impossible without factoring in *magic*.

Jesus was crucified not between two thieves, but two rebels, terrorists. That's a crucial distinction.

He was born into the meanest circumstances, illegitimate, isolated. Endured hardship, incredible tests of his spiritual and mental strength, eventually dying and then, as one apocryphal story recounts, smashing down the gates of Hell, freeing the lost souls inside. The ultimate "rags to riches" story, somewhat hobbled by a central character who seems almost too good to be true.

Showing our pagan roots by always seeking scapegoats.

Wishing I could evince the wisdom of an elder.

Today, I am afflicted by the winter blues.

Eager to shed my Judeo-Christian skin.

History: all our sins remembered.

Is courage innate or learned?
Is cowardice instinctive or acquired?

I want to be less like you.

Behaving myself in front of the cameras.

The same technology behind virtual reality will allow them to read our minds.

We are all data.

Poetry: the last refuge of the narratively disinclined.

The Hereafter: inhabited by far too many people I know.

With each new day, still refusing to acknowledge the ongoing miracle.

Lately, all of my words have been poorly chosen.

From a December 2, 2010 message taped over my desk: "Modest. Respectful, infinitely grateful for the blessings bestowed upon me. Never taking anything in my life for granted. Praising God in word and deed."

The relative innocuousness of a virgin birth in a universe as vast and improbable as ours.

I'm told miracles are fairly commonplace in the event horizon of a black hole (*see*: previous citation).

At what point will the human experiment be discontinued because of budgetary cutbacks?

Fossil fuels: subsisting on the dead.

I have known true love and, so, am blessed.

Time to make a bonfire of my vanity.

James Salter's refusal to adhere to the "arbitrary separation" of fact and fiction. (From his *New York Times* obituary)

To be helpless, immobile, inarticulate.
Worse than death.

Laughter as medicine.
Laughter as a weapon.
In either case, a defense mechanism.

Capable of great evil but *choosing* to do good.

From *Isaiah*: "The people who walked in darkness have seen a great light."

Sometimes Shakespeare is a shitty playwright.

I burned my ships a long time ago, stranding myself on this hostile world.

Capitalism is not a meritocracy.
In fact, the reverse is true.

First contact: in the hurly-burly of our times would we even notice?

Getting above my station, forgetting I am a primate, and not
a very intelligent or distinguished one at that.

Shock doctrine = economic E.C.T.

My mind, a relic of the transistor era.

Time speeded up once we landed on the moon.

When it happens, will we be ready, can anything prepare us
for the horror to come?

Anyone who breathes, eats, defecates, cannot possibly qualify
as a saint.

Struggling to keep pace with the future, one gadget at a time.

Futility doesn't do justice to my situation.

Losing relevance, even during my lifetime.

As obsolete and useless as last year's tech.

A system built around greed will strongly resist scrutiny and regulation.

We are safe here, but for how long?

Most people would've given up ages ago.

Trying to make failure a virtue.

Heads down, mouths shut, docile and mute as we are herded into the abattoir.

Losing my perspective and my sense of humor.
Forgetting how and when to laugh.

Planet #9: huge, invisible, lurking on the periphery of our solar system. Its existence only theoretical, defended by a small but vociferous priesthood.

I have a natural inclination to take offense for the same reason a thumbtack always lands point up.

To possess the courage and conviction of Rosa Luxemburg.

Ignorance: when you don't know.
Stupidity: when you don't *want* to know.

My father would say of someone he detested: "That man is the essence of nothing".

Poetry: the biggest ideas confined to the smallest spaces.

When all else fails, sophistry and *ad hominem* attacks.

When does stubbornness acquire pathological characteristics?

Slavoj Zizek is right, it's better to be a pessimist, that way there's always the possibility of a pleasant surprise.

No gold stars for exemplary behavior.

Mellowing with age, not quite as scornful.

I'll stop believing in the intrinsic decency of the human race when I stop believing in Santa Claus.

Cultivate the image of a harmless eccentric.

Late capitalism: indications of senility, visible signs of decay.

For those who denigrate Plato, Zizek points out that in *Republic*, there are no slaves and women enjoy equal rights.

Dreams of foundations being undermined by leaking water.

Casting a thin line into the roaring *zeitgeist*.

I am a stupid man, struggling to understand.
…and an enigmatic man, struggling to be understood.

It has been conclusively determined that capitalism and
democracy are inimical.

Maybe God isn't dead, but in seclusion, pondering his options.

That last grain of sand, poised to fall through the hourglass.

Have I made a terrible mistake?

Tired of the sound of my voice.

"Man is an animal who needs a master." (Immanuel Kant)
Whether that master be his conscience, God…or Stalin.

Any dedicated, honest observer of our species swiftly becomes
a misanthrope.

Directed to the servants' entrance.

Constantly reminded of my assigned caste.

The enticements of order versus the awful responsibility of freedom.

A *voyant* and therefore not of this earth.

We are a cosmic accident, easily remedied.

The latest in a long line of undiscovered geniuses.

Shame must be earned.

Genial in appearance, venal in spirit.

A fresh crop of cold sores when my immune system is overwhelmed.

Humility and deference toward my superiors.

There was nothing *banal* about Auschwitz.

In the shadows cast by the Holocaust, Rwandan genocide, Srebenica, how can you possibly speak of human ingenuity and progress?

A poet and, therefore, expendable.

Franz Kafka unconsciously anticipated the horrors to come.

The future is never as far away as we think.

Hurry, sundown, end this miserable day.

True faith should enhance and broaden our spiritual perspective, not restrict it with exclusionary dogma and anti-humanistic rhetoric.

We all come from somewhere, each one of us an immigrant, refugee, exile, outsider, seeking a safe harbor, a warm place to lay our heads.

Helpless when confronted by indifference.

Conceived in sin, the humblest roots.

To hate democratically, liberally, without discrimination.

Building our bonfire higher, though the trees are running out.

A spendthrift, wasting my days.

I keep my addictions secret.
No "tell-all" book from me.

"Reform or revolution." (Rosa Luxemburg)
"...or collapse?" (me)

Very adroit, but how long can you keep those balls in the air?

In the end, life wears you down.

Of late, I seem to be less governed by my fears (or am I just resigned).

Out-paced, falling further and further behind.

Revenge, even if it means biding my time.

The deeper into the jungle you venture, the further back in time you go.

Fiercely lonesome.
Defiantly remote.

My parents made me, but God created me.

Seeking inspiration or, barring that, a swift kick in the ass.

A better man than I was ten years ago, but still lacking in modesty.

Apologies for the self-absorption.

What sort of mind could conceive of a "date rape" drug?

No precise definitions, hide behind ambiguity.

Is failure an acquired trait, like blue eyes and alcoholism?

Fortune favors the greedy.

The earth keeps warming up. At what point does it catch fire?

I want this on the record: we knew what we were doing.

Lord, help me overcome a tendency for neediness.

Posthumous: when it no longer matters.

Hello, God, what's new?

Brian Eno can't read music and considers himself a poor musician.

Poetry, soon to be another lost language.

In need of new thresholds of wonder.

When the lights go out for good.

Can you read my writing?

I have a recurring nightmare that people are even dumber than I think.

Two texts that are absolutely word perfect: *The Lord's Prayer* and *Sermon on the Mount*.

Is it sacrilege to yearn for Oz and Shangri-La?

Back in the good, old days, God was known to nurse a grudge.

Sing! Drink! Dance!
What's the alternative?

Stubbing my toe, tripping over my own feet, clumsy as a child.

The act of creation is, in essence, an act of love.

Stoic philosophy distilled: *shit happens, deal with it*.

Mementos, not souvenirs.

E.M. Forster said of C.V. Cavafy that he was a man standing "at an angle to the universe".

I'm happier than I pretend to be.

Guided by quarrelsome, contradictory voices.

Book II

I'd rather be the humblest *zek* than a status-seeking, social-climbing, bourgeois asshole.

Our greatest sin: our refusal to acknowledge our sins.

Laughing in my noose.

Humility: when everything else has been taken from you.

Helpless, denied even a crutch to stand on.

Lies sustain us when the truth becomes too difficult to bear.

Hapless, not hopeless (or helpless).

We *all* have hidden agendas.

So afraid of appearing foolish.

My childhood: a lasting legacy of betrayal and mistrust.

Years ago, I told my wife the motto for my life should read: "Willing to be a failure if only to prove myself right". Still not sure if that's bravado or insanity.

To have someone say of me: *Do you know who that is?*
In a tone of honor, respect.

Adhering to certain codes of conduct, observing the basic civilities.

Yeats never made it anywhere near Byzantium.
He wrote how he *imagined* it.

Life, an uninterrupted series of humiliations.

In the thrall of Fate, a road map with the route already filled in.

Etc.

My grip on reality tenuous at the best of times.

The unshakeable fear that at some point it will all be taken away from me.

Kafka's insistence that "a book must be the axe for the frozen sea within us". Yes, yes, YES.

"Nothing succeeds in reproducing itself as a sense of privilege founded on a false sense of entitlement." (Yanis Varoufakis)

Living on the edge can be dangerous but it also offers the best views.

The world's leading expert on fuck all.

There is so little to recommend me.

Better that the universe is indifferent (unconscious) than hostile (conscious).

Obliged to you (and resentful of it).

Malaise: when lack of inspiration becomes acute.

An overgrown child for a mother.
A raging non-entity for a father.

Abused out of anger and frustration.

I use solitude like a desert mystic: *to escape*.

Coincidence: a confluence of impossibilities.

Honest and sincere, when it suits me.

Increasingly at a loss for words...

Suddenly fearful of our health, mindful of mortality.
(That's what a cancer diagnosis does.)
Questioning my faith, the order of the universe.
(I repeat, that's what a cancer diagnosis does.)

Artists are frustrated gods.

All of a sudden, I'm a Marxist.

Sometimes all you can do is pray.

I've been keeping to the fringes, trying to avoid detection.

Still standing, which means I'm either lucky or blessed,
can't decide which.

Resolved to telling fewer lies.

Losing control, bit by bit.

Rather a spectacular failure than a mediocrity.

Sunday night. Dusk. Stoned. Only a small desk lamp
for illumination. Eno's "Discreet Music" playing.
Blissed out. Entranced.

Our world, a disaster in the making.

Civilization, a misnomer.

Waxing recriminatory
refusing consolation
even if it means
extending my sentence.

How do I redeem all those years of wasted days?

Vain, isolated, self-righteous, fearful of being proved wrong; willing to commit any atrocity to prevent full disclosure.

"Smart" devices, narcing on us to their corporate masters.

I should've been a better husband, father, brother, son.

I say I'm a work-in-progress, you say I'm an accident waiting to happen. Turns out we're *both* right.

To prevent the darkness, in all its cruel guises.

Addiction on every branch and twig of my family tree.

Self-diagnosis: intellectually lazy, morally slippery.

The inanity and superficiality of that which can be bought and owned.

Conceiving of a world where miracles are as commonplace as summer daisies.

The necessity of widening the parameters of my existence.

Drugs, when nothing else works.

An epidemic of suicide in my age group.

In my solitary room, surrounded by listening walls.

A childhood of terrible earaches and cowardly behavior.

The receding taillights as we watched our father fleeing the scene of his crimes.

The departure songs of distant trains.

My childhood hardwired me for fear and anxiety.
I am programmed for flight.

Starving fawn.
Blame God.
Dying child.
No God.

I predict more of the same, only worse.

I still yearn for a robot sidekick.
Non-judgmental; tinny laughter at my weak jokes.

Not fame or notoriety, more like something resembling *respect*.

Graham Hancock refers to Judaism, Christianity and Islam as "Abrahamic death cults".

"Well, it may be the Devil/
and it may be the Lord/
but we all gotta serve somebody."
(Bob Dylan)

What will survive of me?

Old age.
Infirmity.
Death.
No longer laughing matters.

I'm the kind of person who sits in a rundown, pseudo-Irish
pub at 3:30 in the afternoon and immediately feels at home
with the regulars. Soaking up a miasma of slopped booze,
vomit, essence of urinal puck. The bartenders interchangeable,
noted for their dab hand at pouring Guinness.

Drinking: compensatory behavior; a rationale for failure.

Writers in libraries seem respectful, even reverent, but inside
they are *seething* with envy, dubious that many of the books
they're browsing deserve to be there, blatant favoritism and
political correctness rather than sheer talent earning them a
spot on those hallowed shelves, a status forever denied those
toiling day and night on behalf of the printed word, dying
without recognition or acknowledgement.

Life: an interval during which your worst fears are realized.

Love: exposing the paucity of reason.

The circular logic of dogma, the reassuring certainty of cant.

To save the world we require time (and we're a hundred years too late).

My old friend Boredom visiting again today. An annoying, bothersome presence who keeps ignoring me whenever I hint it's time to leave.

Don't be querulous, argumentative, insistent.
Don't mistake their pained expressions for interest.

The lamp turned low, the light of Faith barely registering against the encroaching darkness.

The intention as important as the act.

Context (with accompanying footnotes) is everything.

If we didn't doubt, we wouldn't be worthy of God.

Oh, the crimes I've committed, the indignities I've inflicted in the dark precincts of my mind.

Metaphor originates in the unconscious.

Thomas Pynchon turns eighty.
Allegedly, a regular pot smoker.
Undeniably a genius.
Connection?

Another failed experiment.
Now it's just a case of writing up the notes.

A post-mortem conference involving all the principals.
How could a universe go so spectacularly wrong?

What we call satire is actually veiled contempt.

What comes after absolute zero?

This dumbshow, the utter ridiculousness of it all…

Nothing to contribute.
Furious. Frustrated.
Hopeless. Resigned.

"In order to really suffer, one has to be faithful." (Zbigniew Herbert)

The docility of one who knows the house never loses.

This is what I must do: tend my tiny garden, till, seed,
cultivate, harvest. Concede the world but protect what
little I claim as mine.

A stiff back *used* to mean a good day's work.

I am the last of the least.

Continue my inquiries, wherever they take me.

A degree in superficial knowledge courtesy the university of the internet.

My mindset these days: frustrated disbelief, generalized outrage.

In the final analysis we are alone.
There are places inside us too terrible to share with anyone.

Kind and affable, until you get to know me.

It is impossible to betray a stranger.
True treachery requires intimacy, close association.

Forgotten, gradually fading away.

The past a default setting for when the future loses its promise.

Either serve in gratitude or not at all.

Your choice: rise to the challenge or lower your expectations.

We're *all* whores, providing a service for filthy lucre.

That little notebook Leonard Cohen kept with him, almost to his dying breath.

A life steeped in avoidance: where's the courage in that?

Noir: what the shadows reveal.

Each of us at liberty to invent their own past, fictionalize childhood memories, add color to the pale, grey simulacrum. Don't tell me you've never been tempted to get away with a lie.

The moment they ignite those big rockets, the rumble you feel in your back.

Catharsis, for art's sake (let them see you bleed).

Does surrender mean compliance?
Does acquiescence indicate complicity?
Can passivity absolve us of moral culpability?

For most of us, a "fact" is a subjective interpretation of cherry-picked sources.

A propensity for morbidity dating back to childhood.

Autobiography: self-regard taken to ridiculous extremes.

Some things can't be fixed.

Impending loss: a priceless vase on its way to the floor.

Deathwatch, remorselessly ticking.

You should be able to scrape samples of an author's DNA from their first drafts.

Reflection: a time for doubt and regret.

We always outlive our relevance, that's why death often comes as such a relief.

Archive: purgatory for dead words.

From beyond the footlights, the sound of collective weeping.

"I used to be disgusted/now I try to be amused."
(Elvis Costello)

My life (*cue canned laughter*).

Never before has an author labored so mightily and achieved so little.

The primary difference between humans and "lower animals" is that we believe there must be a reason or purpose for our suffering.

Behaving like prey, frightened of everything.

Eleven hundred wildfires reported in British Columbia this summer. The smoke from burning forests darkening skies from coast to coast.

"Why does an image seen in a mirror appear more beautiful than reality?" (Max Ernst)

An atheist in his foxhole may not pray, but he certainly wishes *devoutly* to be elsewhere.

Water doesn't extinguish fire, it quenches its thirst.

Forever exists outside Time, a transcendent realm poised equidistantly between life and death.

The older I get, the more I realize none of us knows what the hell we are doing—male or female, rich or poor, powerful or weak.

I'll fill these pages even if I have to make shit up.

Write until it's too dark to see.

Persona non grata.
My name struck from the rolls.

"Writing is turning one's worst moments into money."
(J.P. Donleavy)

Half the time people tell only half-truths.

As you age, you get better at lying with a straight face.

I hope my ego fades before my sex drive.

I've lost the narrative thread and exist in a post-modern
nightmare.

Faith = irrational belief + desperate hope.

The stars seem dimmer now.

Yes, I forgive you but that doesn't mean you're absolved.

My inner Ed Gein: a desire to collect and preserve the
corpses of my enemies.

I recoil from prolonged contact with Others, the contagion
I sense there. Preferring my cramped, truncated universe,
doing my best to ignore the importunate pounding on my
reinforced, triple-locked front door.

My father's life and death a warning to those who believe it is possible to thrive without love.

Writers don't make good lovers. After all, there's invariably an alter ego standing off to the side, taking notes, trying to get the texture of our partner's lips and skin just right…

Indulging myself of late, my inner child liberated, bouncing on the expensive furniture.

That selfish little voice inside me that insists the world's problems aren't mine and it's okay to act like I don't care.

What doesn't kill you outright is probably saving you for dessert.

From a *Foo Fighters* song: "Were you born to resist/or be abused?" I know which one *I* choose.

I will translate you into Braille, use soft fingers to read your raised bumps, divine your intentions.

We must remain receptive to any hint of the miraculous.

No river impassable despite its futile torrent.

An addict is the ultimate consumer.

Democracy and *capitalism* are no longer amiable bedfellows. One of them will end up sleeping on the floor.

"The more empty the photograph, the more it will imply horror." (Luc Sante)

Anyone who doesn't believe in evolution should take a good look at what's swinging from their family tree.

I am not my father, but I am just as inclined to hate.

Sobriety is for those who have a bright, shining future.

What do you call it when all hope has been exhausted, inspiration fleeing from you? *Today*.

Life: standup comedy before a hostile audience.

Love has become trivialized.

Can you find anything truly holy in this benighted world?

Does any gospel suffice?

For as long as we've been conscious of our personal extinction we have feared it. Is that what prompted religion? Did we invent gods out of existential dread?

Are any of us innocent or worthy of mercy?

Are you one of those people who proffers gifts in lieu of affection?

Related by blood to neurotic, passive-aggressive, undemonstrative, bitter, suspicious under-achievers.

If this is my fate, I don't see how I've earned it.

Tonight, I feel a distinct lack of perspective (i.e. the walls are closing in).

Memory failing, like a malfunctioning computer.

The god of our fathers is a mass murderer.

These days, Heaven is under-populated.

Lying my way out of trouble and congratulating myself for my ingenuity. (Paraphrasing "Captain Kirk")

Drawing succor from a dry well.

Do only the ruthless or amoral succeed?

When patience no longer appeases (nor love sufficeth).

I've stopped cheering for our species.

Anthropocene: when it became our fault.

Postmodernism has a lot to answer for.

I am absolute dictator of an imaginary kingdom.

Our souls impoverished, begging for a sign.

Love? What's left when the world has accomplished its wicked work.

I'm not the man I used to be but…isn't that a *good* thing?

The narcissism of suicide: self = the world (which must be annihilated)

Is there room for civility and reasoned discourse on a dying, toxic planet?

I'll keep singing my song as long as my lungs have capacity.

T-shirt idea: "Anthropocene: The Farewell Tour"

We were granted free will to fail by our own devices (God eschewing blame).

Heroism must be selfless and instantaneous or it is mere egotism.

Never bow. It's a sign of obeisance.

Why would you rather weep than laugh; fall, than dance?

If you're broken, buy glue.

Remembering Marie Antoinette: the whiteness of her neck, the lack of blue in her blood.

Hello, darkness, you've *never* been a friend.

Nighttime prescriptions and remedies, just to be able to sleep.

How easy it would be not to care.

Sedation numbs the senses but cannot quiet the mind.

What was once a coping mechanism has become a full-blown addiction.

Like a falling climber, you try reassuring yourself that you'll eventually gain a handhold, something to arrest your breathless descent.

I have been a coward most of my life and, therefore, have little to regret.

Reality is in desperate need of an upgrade.

My youthful enthusiasm gone, leaving only a stubborn determination to persevere despite insurmountable odds.

Fanatic: the inability to escape false belief systems.

Not even the latest, certainly not the last.

Gore Vidal once said his favorite words were: *I told you so.*

Old and *New Testaments*, *Qur'an*, *Upanishads*, teachings of Buddha: extended essays on the failings of the flesh.

Alexander the temporarily Great.

"You are the full moon in my window/Celestial daughter betrothed me by Pan." (*for Sherron*)

Subsistence, rather than existence.

Do I have any right to complain?

The Cathars: their admirable piety and fatal disregard for worldly authority.

Heresy: the suppressed Truth.

Anthony Bourdain's "bewilderment of stars".

Did I try hard enough to be kind or was I only pretending?

Is there death after life or is our misery perpetuated?

A bed-wetter, chronic masturbator, stubborn idealist.

They'll never kill the thirteen-year-old inside me.

We are judged by our deeds, no other considerations apply.

My skin breaking out again, yet they insist there's nothing wrong with the air.

Othello = prototypical jealous, violent spouse.

Both laughter and grief produce tears.

To have Tarkovsky's aesthetics and Kubrick's strength of mind.

We are not alone in the universe and fortunate that we remain undiscovered. Can you imagine tyranny and cruelty, but on a *galactic* scale?

Assisted suicide: better a staged withdrawal than submit to humiliation, my forces routed, fleeing in disarray.

I've never deliberately sought to harm someone but through negligence and inaction have still inflicted a great deal of pain.

He's not the first world leader to be bought and paid for.

They always make it look like an accident. Or suicide. "Death by misadventure", when what they really mean is "targeted assassination".

Ostensibly because I had nothing to say.

Hamstrung by poor genetics, crippled with self-doubt.

The killers proceeded into the cathedral through the front entrance, leaving their fear of God outside.

Our Creator currently resides in a dusty, cobwebbed corner of my basement. I tend to him as best I can, attempting to raise his spirits with the occasional half-remembered prayer.

Despite millions of years of evolution, our over-sized brains still seek out the simplest, least elegant solutions.

America, the paranoid.
Armed, dangerous, clinically obese.

They read him his rights from a *very* small card.

Are you afraid?
Why not?

The greatest allure of extremism is its deliberate, stupid simplicity.

Harbinger: when you can see something terrible is about to happen and still don't do anything to prevent it.

Hate: a fruitless expenditure of vital energy, usually directed at the wrong person.

Sibelius was informed he was dying (he wasn't) and spent what he thought were his last few months creating his greatest symphony.

If they told you *your* appointed day and hour, would you feel free and unencumbered or condemned and forsaken?

I wanted to be a hero but shall draw some consolation that at least I wasn't a complete villain.

Apply a tourniquet, stop the bleeding.

Laughter: in celebration and defiance.

Why does everyone talk so quickly these days?

Arthritis: if I lose the use of my fingers will I still retain my voice?

How can God go from being so close to so far away?
(Remember, he wrestled with Abraham and spoke directly
to Moses.)

A ceasefire, not an armistice.

Black holes and depression both swallow light.

Possessed by child-like wonder.

Sustained by love, immunized against all iniquity.

Deny nurturing and affection to animals when they're young
and they're almost certain to develop into asocial, savage beasts.

In the time it takes you to remember you've already got it wrong.

Don't cling to the past, it's an invented lie.
Don't dwell on the present, it's still under construction.
Avoid anticipating the future, it will arrive soon enough.

Escape horrific circumstances only to be told my tormentors
won't be punished? What kind of Faustian bargain is that?

Your cooperation appreciated but not mandatory.

Omniscience: a cold, inhuman perspective.

Is my life merely trivial or downright inconsequential?

Ashamed of my accent, the way it betrays my humble origins.

Willing to entertain the most outlandish notions
(unconditional love, redemption, God).

We're in for it now.

Shut in for the winter, ample opportunity to brood.

Volcano: when Hell flows over.

Dragons, unicorns, the pure of heart (all fictitious creations).

Failing with as much dignity as circumstances permit.

My pathetic, mundane life, a biographer's worst nightmare.

Pursuing inspiration with murderous intent.

Fearful: one word, two very separate and distinct meanings
(both applicable in my case).

A failure at everything but failure.

A dearth of success that *must* be willful.
(Everything is self-inflicted.)

Love between two absolute strangers.

We die alone, even when surrounded by family.

Stocking up on food and water, the news getting worse by the hour.

Something is wrong with the weather.

We become truly old only when we tire of birdsong.

Any belief system offers a placebo effect.

I don't belong to a race or gender, only a species.

Making a difference by the smallest possible increments.

Praxis: when theory no longer suffices.

Crowd-funding the restoration of the picture of Dorian Gray.

Voting: yet another empty ritual.

Refuting Gene Kranz: in my case *success* is not an option.

I ask for a window seat to get a better view of the descent.

Random, not necessarily meaningless.

My sisters and I pretended to be animals so our parents wouldn't notice us.

Assisted suicide: when you can't wait to die.

How can there be faith without the leavening presence of doubt? God, despite all the evidence to the contrary?

Jesus questioned his own divinity, thus proving himself worthy of worship.

Theology: manna for the spirit.

A professional at my chosen vocation, a hobbyist when it comes to life.

When the universe was born, accompanied by Sebald's "Gaussian roar", was there a proud father on hand, passing out cigars?

Nature nurtures (then it kills).

The murder of the Canaanites: God playing favorites or monotheism at its worst?

Distilling all human knowledge and experience into a single book, then proscribing it for wanton heresy.

Great religious texts are notorious for their salacious content.

Death: saving the best part 'til the end.

God: the invention of an ambitious species vain enough to claim divine origins.

Salvaging the things we hold most dear, abandoning the rest to the scavengers.

The entire universe is a singularity, an unlikelihood wrapped in an enigma.

Lust and thunder: an excitement of atoms.

No more revelations (God has quit the game).

Given the impossibility of hope, we must rely on prayer.

Jesus was a lapsed Catholic.

Communism: bureaucracy taken to extremes.

Prayer: a collect call where the recipient routinely refuses charges.

A myth is a story so good it must be passed on.

Each one of us should be forced to take the equivalent of a Hippocratic Oath.

The *Old Testament* is a covenant, the *New* an accommodation with earthly powers.

The Edict of Milan: recognizing only compliant faiths.

The sting of a Judas kiss.

Universal monsters: immediately recognizable, common to every culture; tropes and archetypes as ancient as dreams.

Japanese cinema: frustrating the conceits of time.

Western societies are composed of compulsive self-harmers.

Stoicism: in opposition to despair.

The Serenity Prayer: Stoicism's equivalent to the Sermon on the Mount.

Should we be helpless hostages to the impersonal cruelty of the markets?

Marxism is a critique, *not* an ideology.

Capitalism's main contradiction?
It's misanthropic.

Futuresong: "So long, it's been good to know you…"

If I failed, it's because I didn't try hard enough.

Faith should expand your horizons, not contract them.
Your belief should remove all blinders, filters and walls.
Nothing should prevent you from experiencing the undiluted
wonder and majesty of Creation.

When I think about what it means to be an author, *circa*
2020, the analogy I most often use is that I feel like a horse
and buggy salesman watching the first Model "T" rattling by.
Obsolete, out of date. Redundant.

Sadness: what happens when you lose your sense of humor.

Why is so-called "populism" frequently undemocratic and hate-filled?
Are the *demos* inherently vile? Does any large group of people
automatically constitute a mob?

I no longer put my faith in humanity. Too often I have
been disappointed. We work against the common good and
conspire with our masters to preserve the status quo.

Elections: when the farcical nature of democracy is exposed.
(Every four years another roster of collaborators to choose from.)

Blood pressure elevated this morning.
Anticipating the work to come.

What else do you want to know about me? I am
unrepentantly (and irredeemably) Far Left, and if I had my
way rich motherfuckers would pay through the nose and
everyone would consider it a human right to have a fulfilling
trade or profession, a decent wage, all their basic needs
satisfied, their gifts fully utilized, their spirits unbound.

I'm fifty-six years old.
Officially past the "I don't give a shit" threshold.

In my childhood home it was Hallowe'en every single day.

J.G. Ballard ▪ literary terrorist.

The provocateur asks questions, the wise man provides answers.

If you describe a scene set five minutes in the future, you are
writing science fiction.

In an infinite universe there are myriad probabilities, but
no certainty.

Memory is a poorly lit street blanketed by ground fog, icy and
treacherous to navigate.

Is my literary career (thirty+ years and counting) one long vanity project?

Parents must take responsibility for everything so their children remain blameless.

I agree that when employing satire and edgy humor it's preferable to punch *up* rather than *down*. But I also think we owe it to ourselves to speak honestly and forthrightly to *everyone*, powerful or not. To do otherwise would be condescending to certain populations or sub-strata of society. In terms of minority groups and those seeking social justice, it's important to offer perspective, clear-eyed analysis, so they don't become narcissistic, sanctimonious and, worst of all, self-pitying. The truth tends to hurt, no matter who is on the receiving end.

Further the above: "The habit of dwelling on victimhood dulls the impulse of self-correction." (Timothy Snyder, *On Tyranny*)

Melancholy is equal parts sadness and nostalgia.

Words. That's why I'm here, that's what's gotten me into this mess.

Drunk writing: like sexting a complete stranger.

Saying capitalism isn't conducive with democracy is like saying Jack the Ripper had a problem with women.

Somebody, *please*, provide some context.

Obliged, but not beholden.

"Better Down-Loaded Than Dead!"

Fame: when you no longer recognize the person they say you are.

All we make of this is all there is.

How do you monetize willful intransigence?

How do you commodify genuine eccentricity?

The acoustics in Agamemnon's crypt are perfect.

In the final analysis, Kafka, for unflinchingly portraying our helplessness in the face of insurmountable, monolithic forces. (He used to laugh uproariously when reading his work out loud to friends.)

Anxiety is a relatively recent phenomenon.

Stripped of our illusions, our faith, subsisting on ashes, dry remnants of a half-remembered past.

Even Biblical justice did not deter.

I live, therefore I am complicit.
Blameworthy because I was born.

Authentic fairy tales don't have happy endings.

Impressionism was invented by near-sighted artists.

Hate requires effort.
Love demands surrender.

Why do we ignore that inner voice?
Who are we to resist the imperatives of conscience?

Sometimes only a kiss bridges the gap.

Sing, and when words fail you, *hum*.

Guilt: when you choose not to remember.

There is no such thing as non-fiction or documentary; any
observation is inexorably marred by subjectivity and bias.

Pain is the offspring of experience.

The glitches are becoming too obvious to ignore.

Struggling to orient myself amid a roaring cascade of illogic
and ignorance.

March, when winter becomes truly insufferable.

Like winter, some guests linger far too long.

It's not getting better, or easier.
I still struggle for meaning.
Faith eludes me.
Will I die uncomprehending and, thus, in vain?

A singular lack of civility; shouting to make ourselves heard.

John Keats didn't think much of *safe places*. In a letter to his siblings, he wrote: "Do you not see how necessary a world of Pain and troubles is to school an Intelligence and make it a soul? A Place where the heart must feel and suffer in a thousand diverse ways." (Is it possible he wrote those lines while slowly suffocating from tuberculosis?)

You're perfect the way you are, flaws and all.

I will never grasp the American mindset when it comes to possessing guns. Are they insecure because their republic was built on the proceeds of criminal behavior? Do they secretly suspect the people they destroyed or enslaved will one day knock on the front door, asking for their country back?

When isolated, we draw comfort from echoes.

It's quite simple: the capitalists and their stooges *want* us divided into separate enclaves of class, race, gender, identity. The more self-contained silos we build to exclude others, the less likely we are to act collectively to overthrow the oligarchs stealing the country from beneath our feet. The longer we cling to our narcissistic mindsets, the more difficult it will become to resist the social order the uber-wealthy are unilaterally imposing on our dying world.

There is no immunity from the things we feel, that we take in through our six senses. Eventually the filters and buffers fail, leaving us overwhelmed, inundated, crushed by the weight of experience.

I don't like *certainty* and its ugly stepsister *complacency*. They are illusory, offering only temporary shelter from doubt, the towering waves threatening to capsize and engulf us.

Sometimes it takes a thousand ships and many years of bloody conflict to satisfy the whims of Fate.

Trivializing my ruminations by writing them down.

My heartfelt condolences for your manifest idiocy.

Your attention dribbling away like a handful of water.

Disdain is not hate, just like indifference should not be confused with disapproval.

A lie is permissible only if the alternative is worse.

Remorse: weeping in a spreading puddle of spilled milk.

The night before the world ends, I'll be reading.
Poetry, not theology.
God occupying the breaths between spaces.

Help for those who need it.
Punishment for those who deserve it.

If you furiously lash out at someone for expressing an opinion
contrary to your own, it's a sure sign you're peering out from
some rabbit hole and lack the means and temperament to
formulate a response that is both reasonable and cogent.

Love is not a meritocracy.
I did not deserve you and remain baffled by your devotion.
What keeps you from leaving?
What worthiness do you detect in me that I don't?

Little bird, I can't see you well enough to thank you by name
for your gorgeous song.

The tireless industry of a honeybee, undeterred by the
stubborn indifference of the rose.

That sound you make only for me.

You are that place right next to Heaven.

Nature: a melody or cacophony, depending on your state of mind.

There is a terrifying fervency to hate these days, and too many conditions attached to love.

When God dreams, his unconscious gives birth to crib death, the Holocaust, leukemia and mosquitos.

We cannot choose our parents, but we *can* choose to forgive them.

Why do crows always seem to be laughing?

Before the world changed it wasn't any better.

We've stopped listening and so we're no longer heard.

I am suspicious of anyone who doesn't closely examine their motives and biases. We must be our own most stern, relentless critics, vigilant to the point of self-loathing.

Conceived in hope, born into despair.

Halfway to Heaven, trying to enjoy the ride.

On your death bed, yearning for a kiss.

The last straw was three fucking haystacks ago.

We make up stories because we resent being confounded by Mystery.

If it's cold, turn up the heat.
If it's dark, put on a light.

Love is specific and discerning.
It doesn't make mistakes.
Sadly, you have been taken in by mere infatuation.
A bright sun burning your eyes.

Don't forget, the universe is mainly dark matter.

Something tells me you're a true believer, it might be the way your eyes glow.

We prefer being marionettes to the concept of free will.

A punk rocker, despite the crewcut and excellent personal hygiene.

My younger self was an idiot and I wish I could go back in time and tell him so. Of course, when I'm older I'll be more tolerant and will regret a display of churlishness directed toward someone who clearly didn't know better.

The accumulated injuries our bodies and spirits endure in the name of experience.

Cancel culture: allowing no room for regret.

I've grown accustomed (*attached?*) to my faults.

Never before has our species collectively shuddered as we direct our gaze toward the future.

When you kill hope, what's left is *blame*.

A superhero is a god with a backstory.

A writer is similar to a lower order deity in that both are imperfect, jealous, arrogant and inconstant. Neither is worthy of the power of Creation, disqualified for being presumptuous enough to apply.

The devil in the details, concealed by fine print and legalese.

Dialectics have taught me that societies emerge out of a clash of ideas; by ignoring or suppressing dissenting voices we rob ourselves of that special friction and thus confine ourselves to "echo chambers" that endlessly reproduce our tiresome certainty.

Why do old men always become reactionaries?

Long, fallow months sustained only by a thin diet of faint hope.

The glass of life now more than half empty.
From now on, every drop counts.

Prophecy: a prediction that may or may not be divinely inspired.

If the future really is mass extinction, a toxic dystopia of our
own making, only *denial* grants us the ability to throw back
the covers each and every morning, plant our feet firmly on
the floor, rise to confront yet another day.

A good day: not dread, more like anxious anticipation.

Upon being born into this world, our first instinct is to *weep*.

I had fallen out of favor with God and was looking for an
acceptable substitute.

The aquifer beneath the Tree of Life is polluted.

Only old men sing the praises of autumn.

My feelings feigned, heartfelt.

I believe if your faith is too fixed, certain, a kind of complacent
smugness can creep in, a self-congratulatory aspect that denies
the value of doubt and instead embraces a blinkered fanaticism
detrimental to a healthy, magnanimous spirit.

I'm broken but don't want to be fixed; leave me to my infirmities, I count them before I sleep.

I guess I'm growing old but have yet to see any evidence of maturity.

I suppose in the final analysis I'm a poet; through metaphor we apprehend the divine.

I've been cursed with a sense of the absurd since childhood. It has prevented me from respecting authority figures or following any specific school of thought or belief system. For that, I am immensely grateful.

Sometimes comedians and satirists make us cringe.
That's their *job*.

There is a hierarchy of art.
There is a literary pecking order.
If you disagree, you probably don't appear on either.

Let me find comfort in solitude, *o, Lord*, even as the multitudes assail me with clamorous discord.

Reluctant as Jonah.
Doubting as Thomas.
Inconstant as Peter.
Untrustworthy as Judas.
Imperfect as David.
Long-suffering as Job.

It is our capacity to absorb and assimilate pain that determines our mental health, the state of our sanity.

Happiness is unsustainable, sadness inconsolable.

The soul is a sub-atomic particle of Creation.

I used to be a catastrophist, now I can't be bothered. Let's have an end to cares and worries, cease pretending our lives have the slightest significance. Embrace the arbitrary interventions of chance, mutation, luck. Know that you are Sisyphus, your existence purposeless, your heroic exertions objectively foolish and inconsequential (and all the more admirable when seen in that light).

A docent in a museum in the distant future, pointing out some nondescript artifact, assuring her charges it used to indispensable, ubiquitous.

There are countless instructional videos available on how to be better, happier people, each as helpful and authoritative as the next.

One day I shall have to burn my precious library for heat.

The first human communications preserved in carved stone are business transactions and tax records.

There are virtually no original manuscripts in the Kafka Museum in Prague.

Bleeding letters, hemorrhaging vowels and consonants.

Humanity: a noun and an epithet.

You wrote me long letters in lemon juice, invisible and bitter…

The telescope revealed how small we are.

I don't know what's worse, getting older or no longer feeling young.

In a fast-spreading infinitude does it matter if we succeed or fail? Are we not indistinguishable, inconsequential, even in the all-knowing eyes of a sympathetic god?

No gods, only false idols.
No demons, only cruelty without purpose.

One should not romanticize childhood—there is nothing sentimental about a learning curve so steep, it can permanently cripple the unwary.

The contrarian inside me, resisting all methods of coercion, every attempt to impose the hegemony of consensual reality.

When I've killed the sunshine and summoned toxic rain.

I aspire to write the forever song.

Raping and murdering Mother Earth, the ultimate Oedipal act.

I'd give up, but what's the point?

Life: a Ouija Board where the planchette always hovers over "No".

Tomorrow means forever, yesterday another regret being born.

There are billions of ways of looking at the world,
not one of them definitive but each, in their own way,
truthful and authentic.

Red: history's favorite color.

In my work (my small-a "art"), a strong moral center
definitely exists, it just refuses to assert itself.

Solitary individuals cultivate a specific sort of eccentricity
that others might understandably mistake for genius. The
loneliest among us are the most inspired and, it must be
said, the most dangerous.

Stewards, when convenient.
Despoilers, out of sheer habit.

Disembodied thoughts, afterimages of some traumatic
memory no amount of therapy or drugs can diminish.

A carapace is what's left after all the soft inner meat and organs have been removed; a brittle, polished skeleton, preserved for public exhibition, pierced by dull pins.

So besotted with ourselves we can't imagine being extinct, nothing left but a puzzling, contradictory fossil record and tree rings that speak of an epoch of disaster and strife.

Autocracy: when democracy ceases being relevant and privacy something our parents had, the reason they kept their bedroom door closed.

Harried by a conscience that refuses to allow for time served, my sins still freshly made, face scalded with shame.

A skeptic, not a cynic.
The difference between disbelief and nihilism.

Haruspex: I've examined my own entrails and determined there will be much hardship and tribulation in my life for the foreseeable future.

Some terrible recollection of the future, a memory waiting to be born.

Atrocity: shocking, but rarely unexpected.

I'll keep this to myself, my own private grudge.

They want to restrict or limit vocabulary.
They want to own the high ground.
Controlling methods of discourse.
Screaming when they don't get their way.

The person in the mirror: does your much-vaunted capacity
for forgiveness extend to *them*?

Counting down the years, months, days, hours…
An hourglass and its inexorable cascade of descending sand.

They call it "chronic" pain, because it never ends.

We strive for posterity but all we leave behind are traces.

Even my own modest lifestyle is unsustainable. We must learn
to make do with less and not regard it as an unjust punishment.

Who am I? What is my identity?
The sum total of my deeds.

The storyline they're advancing very old, very effective, the
tactics familiar, their motivations manifestly obvious.

Stop looking for saviors when a single honest man will do.

Straining for the sound of another human voice.

It's not that I disbelieve you, it's just that I think you're dead wrong.

We make our own universes and create our own heavens.

I stopped demanding answers and, instead, begged for meaning.

You and I: a confluence, perfect harmony.

"When paradigms collide!"

The last Cathar, unrepentant and willingly commended to the flames.

I've started forgetting all I have learned, knowledge trickling away. Soon I'll be as stupid and helpless as a child.

Age erodes desire, replacing it with comforting nostalgia.

Fear and want make for an anxious and angry citizenry.

If we were truly ignorant, we might have an excuse.

If all your prayers are being answered, you're not asking for enough.

If wishes were horses, I'd be Roy Rogers.

Isolation: not punishment or privation, but an opportunity to find out who you really are.

Intoxicants, because I fear boredom most of all.

A gift for annoying people or a valuable strategy for preserving my autonomy?

I have loved and been loved and therefore am blessed.

Rendered legless by a kiss.

They play off emotions, buzz words, kneejerk reactions. Appealing to the reptile brain, bypassing the frontal lobes.

Van Morrison, "No Guru, No Method, No Teacher". *Exactly*.

I pace constantly to present a moving target.

Too many sob stories these days, too many people insisting on the primacy of their pain.

The darker it gets, the more I like it.

The so-called "State" is *us*.

Universality vs. Individualism.
(The future depends on it.)

Is it worse to know you're not free, or to foolishly cling to the belief you are?

We only have so much bandwidth.
Saving the planet must take precedence.
All other causes and agendas off the table until we determine whether or not our species survives the next hundred years.

Oligarchy: when participatory democracy founders.

Percussion: the original sound.

Love sustains even as the world falls apart around us.

My published work: the astonishing breadth of my ignorance and incompetence laid bare.

I survive in order to testify.
I exist to bear witness.
I persevere so that I may explain.
Achieving dotage for the purpose of atonement.

Inevitable as Fate or random as a wayward atom?
Isn't each equally terrifying?

I don't know who "I" am.
Small wonder I'm so bewildered by "you".

I think there's a sick, demented part of me that seeks and maybe even *desires* failure, craving the consolation that accompanies a truly catastrophic turn of events.

Misanthrope about covers it.

Good morning, death is now officially one day closer.

In lieu of tomorrow, would you be willing to settle for a promissory note?

If these *are* the End Times, our sorry circumstances are entirely of our own devising. No supernatural intrigues or *deus ex machina* required.

Have we failed the future, or has *it* failed *us*?

A common language permits a collective warning shout: *the enemy approacheth!*

Evil is timeless, deathless and terrifyingly persuasive.

I shall never submit to the blandishments of the literal, the virtual, the false narratives and creation myths that sustain so many. Let us have *truth*, above all else, put an end to reassuring lies.

Divine love requires no reciprocity and does not rely on the vicissitudes of belief.

Extinct before we even knew it.
Our death rattle a *cri de coeur* echoing in the corridors of time.

A victim is never complicit.
A survivor need not forgive.

The love that dare not hold its silence.

The courage it takes to resist.

I did the best I could, taking into account the substandard material I had to work with.

Horror becomes us.

Farewell, which does not necessarily mean *good-bye*.

Cliff Burns has been an independent author and publisher for over three decades. He has written fifteen books and his work has appeared in publications and anthologies around the world. He lives in western Canada with his wife, artist and educator Sherron Harman Burns.